Kissing in Kansas City
A Romantic Discovery Tour

by Peter Mallouk

ADDAX
PUBLISHING
GROUP

Published by Addax Publishing Group
Copyright © 1998 by Peter Mallouk
Designed by Randy Breeden
Cover Design by Jerry Hirt

For Information address:
Addax Publishing Group
8643 Hauser Drive, Suite 235, Lenexa, KS 66215

Library of Contress Cataloging-in-Publication Data

Mallouk, Peter, 1970-
    Kissing in Kansas City / by Peter Mallouk.
        p.   cm.
    ISBN 1-886110-47-6
    1. Kansas City (Mo.)—Guidebooks. 2. Kissing—Missouri—Kansas
City—Guidebooks. I. Title.
    F474.K23M35   1998
    917.78'4110443—dc21   97-51143
                                                               CIP

ISBN: 1-886110-47-6

Distributed to the trade by Andrews McMeel
4520 Main Street
Kansas City, MO 64111

1 3 5 7 9 10 8 6 4 2
Printed in the United States of America

For Veronica,
who keeps me thinking romantic thoughts.

"A kiss is a lovely trick designed by nature to stop speech when words become superfluous."

Ingrid Bergman

Acknowledgments

This book is the finished product of many short days and long nights. A great deal of assistance from many went into the making of this book. Al Pitzner, the primary photographer for this project, did an excellent job of working within my seemingly unrealistic framework. The enthusiasm, expertise, and flexibility he brought to the project helped make it a successful reality. John Siebs' photographs are some of the most creative, and I thank him for stepping in at the eleventh hour to help make this happen. Gary Carson also contributed photographs, including the cover shot. His help in bringing this project from the drawing board to the bookshelf was invaluable. Veronica Yaghmour, my fiancee, worked with me on almost every phase of the project, from finding and selecting quotes, writing copy, and helping with the photo shoots. I would also like to single out my mom, Carmen Mallouk, for her ideas and input, especially regarding photography. Bret Davis, a great friend, came through for me on many occasions. I would especially like to thank him for his last second help lining up models, and for filling in at times. Many others warrant thanks, including Bob Snodgrass, and Darcie Kidson at Addax, both contributed ideas and many hours to this project. Thanks to the many models in this book. I would especially like to express my gratitude to those that contributed their time on several occasions: Mike Smoots, Tanya Wilson, Mike and Annie Flynn, Steve Hodes, Neysa Brooks, Michelle Rottering, Rick Jaso, Kim Bellome, Bobby Ngo, Rance Ames and Monica Frohok. I appreciate the time you took out of your busy schedules, as well as your patience and help.

Foreword

"What do you want to do?"
"I don't know. What do you want to do?"

How often have you and your significant other had a conversation that started like the previous statements..

Or maybe this sounds familiar….

"Well, I can't decide because there's nothing to do around here."
"Yeah, I guess we'll just go to another movie/rent another movie."

This book is about putting conversations like those above to rest for a long, long time. There is far more to do in Kansas City than just go to dinner and a movie, although Kansas City is home to some of the best restaurants in the country, some of which are in this book.

But, Kansas City is home to much more than that! Kansas City offers some of the finest museums in the nation like the Nelson Art Gallery, a totally revamped zoo (when was the last time you went there?), several theme parks, one of the best shopping districts in the country, and five river boat casinos.

Kansas City is also home to several beautiful parks like Loose Park and Shawnee Mission Park , taverns like the Velvet Dog and Harry's Bar and Tables, and spectacular events like the Renaissance Festival, the Plaza Art Fair, the American Royal Bar-B-Q, and every Chiefs home game.

When was the last time you spent a day shopping, walking, and eating at the Country Club Plaza, Westport, or Crown Center? Have you ever seen the Kansas City Symphony, gone skating at the Crown Center ice skating rink, or been at the Plaza when the lights actually came on Thanksgiving night? And have you heard of the River Market but don't really know what it's all about?

There are many ways to see all Kansas City has to offer. How about a walk on the Plaza, a walk along Brush Creek, maybe a Trolley ride, or perhaps a ride in a horse-drawn-carriage? No matter what your selection, you are sure to see some beautiful scenery, statues, and of course fountains. There is a reason Kansas City is called the City of Fountains.

Of course, this book can't possibly cover everything there is to do with your date in Kansas City. This book is designed to serve as a starting point, a place to get a new idea every now and then. You take it from there. So, in short, no more excuses! Next time you have free time think twice before doing the same old thing. There is a lot more to do in Kansas City than you ever thought!

Performing Arts are alive and well in Kansas City. The *Kansas City Symphony* gives regular performances from fall to spring at the Lyric Theater. The *Lyric Opera of Kansas City*, the oldest performing arts organization in Kansas City, presents opera as theater in English. The *State Ballet of Missouri* performs original contemporary and classical ballet, including its popular annual production of "The Nutcracker." Every summer, Broadway shows and concerts constantly stream through Kansas City's premier amphitheater, the *Starlight Theater*. If you're looking for current Broadway musicals and comedies, check out the *New Theater Restaurant*, which pairs entertainment with gourmet dining.

Kansas City Symphony: Lyric Theater, 11th & Central   816-471-0400
Lyric Opera of Kansas City: Lyric Theater, 11th & Central   816-471-7344
State Ballet of Missouri: 1228 Main St.   816-932-2232
Starlight Theater: Swope Park, near Meyer Blvd. & Swope Pkwy 816-333-9481
New Theater Restaurant: 9229 Foster   913-649-0123

*"The moment eternal - just that and no more -
When ecstasy's utmost we clutch at the core
While cheeks burn, arms open, eyes shut, and lips
meet!"*

Robert Browning

State Ballet of Missouri

"Love doesn't make the world go round. Love is what makes the world worthwhile."

Franklin P. Jones

"People who are sensible about love are incapable of it."

Douglas Yates

Kansas City Symphony

Attractions abound in Kansas City. The historic *City Market* is home to the largest farmer's market in five states, gift shops, restaurants, galleries, the Arabia Steamboat Museum, and countless events. If the Market is not your thing, head out to the "country." *Benjamin Ranch* on the Santa Fe Trail is a western ranch in the middle of the city. It offers horseback and pony rides, hayrides, and country entertainment. Want an excuse to drink with your beau? Take a tour through *Boulevard Brewery Company*, a local brewery that offers free tours on Saturdays. When you've got a full day to enjoy, head out to *Worlds of Fun*, Kansas City's premier theme park offers over 140 rides, including the Timberwolf, ranked as one of the top roller coasters in the world. If the weather is nice, visit *Oceans of Fun*, the Midwest's largest water park. When was the last time you went to the *Kansas City Zoo*? Now is the time to try something different. Check out the new animals, exhibits, attractions, and IMAX theater. If gambling is your thing, Kansas City is the place to be. Kansas City is home to five casinos: *Harrah's, Station Casino, Argosy Riverside, The Flamingo*, and *Sam's Town*.

City Market: 5th St., between Wyandotte & Grand	816-842-1271
Benjamin Ranch: I-435 & E. 87th St.	816-765-1100
Boulevard Brewery Company: 2501 Southwest Blvd.	816-474-7095
Worlds of Fun: I-435, exit 54	816-454-4545
Oceans of Fun: I-435, exit 54	816-454-4545
Kansas City Zoo: I-435 & 63rd St.	816-871-5700
Harrah's: Highway 210 & Chouteau Trafficway	816-472-7777
Station Casino: 8201 NE Birmingham Rd.	816-453-7303
Argosy Riverside: I-635 & Highway 9	816-746-7711
Flamingo: 1800 E. Front St.	816-855-7777
Sam's Town: 6711 NE Birmingham Rd.	816-414-7777

Worlds of Fun

"Love is a canvas furnished by Nature and embroidered by imagination."

Voltaire

"Life has taught us that love does not consist in gazing at each other but in looking outward together in the same direction."

Antoine de Saint-Exupery

River Market

"One word frees us of all the weight and pain in life. That word is love."

Sophocles

"By all means marry. If you get a good wife you will become happy, and if you get a bad one you will become a philosopher."

Socrates

Flamingo Casino

"Now join your hands, and with your hands your hearts."

William Shakespeare,
King Henry the Sixth

*"For you see, each day I love you more,
today more than yesterday and less than
tomorrow."*

Rosemonde Gerard

Kansas City Zoo

Sports fans have many choices, and surely there must be at least one which you and your significant other can both enjoy. *Chiefs* fever has had Kansas City under its spell over the last several years. Football can't be romantic you say? Tell that to all the men who have surprised their girlfriends in front of 78,000 fans via overhead planes dragging wedding proposals! The Kansas City *Royals* offer the perfect excuse to spend an evening under the stars. Kansas City is also home to the *Wiz* (outdoor soccer), the *Attack* (indoor soccer), the *Blades* (hockey), and the *Explorers* (tennis).

Chiefs: Arrowhead Stadium, I-70 & Blue Ridge Cutoff	816-931-3330
Royals: Kauffman Stadium, I-70 & Blue Ridge Cutoff	816-422-1969
Wiz: Arrowhead Stadium, I-70 & Blue Ridge Cutoff	816-472-4625
Attack: Kemper Arena, 1800 Genessee	816-474-BALL
Blades: Kemper Arena, 1800 Genessee	816-842-5233
Explorers: American Royal Complex's Hale Arena	913-362-9944

"For twas not into my ear you whispered, but into my heart. Twas not my lips you kissed, but my soul."

Judy Garland

Arrowhead Tailgate Party

"It is love, not reason, that is stronger than death."

Thomas Mann

Love seeketh not itself to please,
Nor for itself hath any care,
But for another gives it ease,
And builds a Heaven in Hell's despair.

William Blake

Parks offer Kansas Citians a place to take it easy. *Swope Park*, the second largest city park in the nation, offers a golf course, picnic shelters, guided nature trail hikes, nature science programs, swimming, and plenty of trees. *Shawnee Mission Park* offers camping facilities, trails, athletic fields, and a place sectioned off just for dogs (the *"Dog Park"*). The observation tower provides a beautiful view of the area, including the 150-acre lake. *Loose Park* sits on the site of the Civil War Battle of Westport. However, Loose Park is definitely a favorite of lovers, not fighters, as its *Rose Garden* is a favorite location for marriage proposals and weddings. *Smithville Lake*, a 7,200 acre lake that offers swimming, sailing, beaches, and fishing, is surrounded by parks offering camping, hiking trails, a public golf course, picnic sites, and much more. Other area favorites include *Blue Springs Lake, Longview Park & Lake*, and *Penn Valley Park*.

Swope Park: Swope Pkwy & Meyer Blvd.	816-444-3113
Shawnee Mission Park: 79th & Renner Blvd.	913-831-3355
Loose Park: 51st & Wornall	816-561-9710
Smithville Lake: Highway 9, 2.2 miles east of U.S. 169	816-532-0803
Blue Springs Lake: 1 mile east of Highway 291 on Bowlin Rd.	816-795-1112
Longview Park & Lake: Longview Rd., off Raytown Rd.	816-795-8200
Penn Valley Park: South from Pershing between Main & Southwest Trafficway	

"Love one another and you will be happy. It is as simple and as difficult as that."

Michael Leunig

Swope Park

"Caresses, expressions of one sort or another, are necessary to the life of the affections as leaves are to the tree of life."

Nathaniel Hawthorne

"A very small degree of hope is sufficient to cause the birth of love."

Stendhal

Loose Park

"I think you're supposed to get shot with an arrow or something, but the rest of it isn't supposed to be painful."

Manuel, age 8

"An act of love that fails is just as much a part of the divine life as an act of love that succeeds, for love is measured by fullness, not by reception."

Harold Loukes

Shawnee Mission Park

Fountains & Statues can be found throughout the Kansas City area. Kansas City is often called the City of Fountains. Some have become part of the essence of Kansas City, like the *Meyer Circle Fountain*. The *J.C Nichols Memorial Fountain*, on the Plaza, has become a Kansas City landmark. It was dedicated to the developer of the Plaza. The four heroic horsemen in the fountain represent the rivers of the world. The statues were sculpted in Paris in 1910, and installed in 1960. The Plaza also boasts statues from around the world. One of the more popular is the *Married Love* statue that depicts Sir Winston and Lady Churchill. If you like what you see, a good starting point to find more is, of course, the Plaza, which has over 50 beautiful fountains and statues.

"A compliment is like a kiss through a veil."

Victor Hugo

Crown Center Fountain

"Neither a lofty degree of intelligence nor imagination nor both together go to the making of genius. Love, love, love, that is the soul of genius."

Wolfgang Amadeus Mozart

"Love cures people, both the ones who give it and the ones who receive it."

Dr. Karl Menninger

Married Love

"We love because it's the only true adventure."

Nikki Giovanni

"Love is the greatest miracle cure. Loving ourselves works miracles in our lives."

Louise Hay

Meyer Circle Fountain

"Life is the flower for which love is the honey."

Victor Hugo, French novelist

"Who, being loved, is poor?"

$\mathscr{Oscar\ Wilde}$

Diana Fountain

"The love we give away is the only love we keep."

Elbert Hubbard

"To love someone deeply gives you strength. Being loved by someone deeply gives you courage."

Unknown

The Boar

"This is the miracle that happens every time to those who really love; the more they give, the more they possess."

Rainer Maria Rilke

"The lover knows much more about absolute good and universal beauty than any logician or theologian, unless the latter, too, be lovers in disguise."

George Santayana

J.C. Nichols Memorial Fountain

Festivals are prevalent in Kansas City. It seems like there is always one taking place. Every July, the *Jazz and Blues Festival* celebrates Kansas City's great jazz tradition. Kansas City's biggest festival, *The Spirit Festival*, is an annual celebration featuring hundreds of local and regional bands representing every genre imaginable. The Spirit Festival also features several national acts, hundreds of vendors, great food, and a carnival. The *Ethnic Enrichment Festival* celebrates Kansas City's diverse culture with entertainment and food that cover the globe. Spend the day with he one you love in Canterbury! Every year the *Renaissance Festival* has new shows, great food, and over 150 artisans, all harking back to the 16th century. They even have a Renaissance chapel, where couples marry (for real!) in a truly royal ceremony. The *Heart of America Shakespeare Festival* offers free Shakespeare performances in Southmoreland Park in July. A favorite of partygoers, the annual *American Royal BBQ*, is one of Kansas City's most popular events.

Jazz and Blues Festival	800-530-5266
Spirit Festival: Penn Valley Park	816-221-4444
Ethnic Enrichment Festival	816-842-7530
Renaissance Festival: I-70, Bonner Springs exit	816-561-8005
Shakespeare Festival: 47th & Oak	816-531-7728
American Royal BBQ & Rodeo	816-221-9800

"A kiss is a pleasant reminder that two heads are better than one."

Unknown

American Royal Barbeque

"It is with true love as it is with ghosts; everyone talks about it, but few have seen it."

Francois de La Rouchefoucauld

"If you judge someone, you have no time to love them."

Mother Teresa

Renaissance Festival

Restaurants in Kansas City have earned their reputation for excellence. The American Restaurant, EBT, Café Allegro, The Peppercorn Duck Club, and Skies have all been voted as some of the most romantic restaurants in Kansas City by readers of Ingrams magazine. The *American Restaurant* offers the perfect ambiance for a romantic dinner for two. This four star restaurant with a marvelous view of Kansas City serves fine American cuisine. If you're in the mood for a garden-like setting, *EBT* is the perfect choice. For a change of pace, try the eclectic seasonal entrees of a local favorite, *Café Allegro. The Peppercorn Duck Club*, known for its delectable desserts, offers a more formal setting and gourmet menu. Whether it's dinner or just drinks, nothing compares to the view of Kansas City from *Skies* rotating rooftop restaurant. *Café Sebastienne*, located in the Kemper Museum of Contemporary Art and Design, is one of Kansas City's newer restaurants and has already developed an avid following. The restaurant itself is as beautiful as the museum in which it is located. *Classic Cup*, a Plaza favorite, offers contemporary cuisine in a European bistro setting and one of the finest wine lists in the city. Of course, Kansas City's restaurant tradition cannot be done justice by this brief overview, so whether barbecue or more elegant fare is your taste, Kansas City offers many choices for you and your date.

The American Restaurant: Crown Center, 25th & Grand   816-426-1133
EBT: 1310 Carondelet (I-435 & State Line)   816-942-8870
Café Allegro: 1815 W. 39th St.   816-561-3663
The Peppercorn Duck Club: Hyatt Regency, 2345 McGee   816-421-1234
Skies: Hyatt Regency, 2345 McGee   816-421-1234
Café Sebastienne: 4420 Warwick Blvd, inside the Kemper Museum   816-561-7740
Classic Cup: 301 W. 47th St.   816-753-1840

*"There is the kiss of welcome and
of parting, the long lingering, loving,
present one; the stolen or the mutual one;
the kiss of love, of joy, and of sorrow;
the seal of promise and receipt of fulfillment."*

Thomas Haliburotn

Café Sebastienne

"Better to have loved and lost, than to have never loved at all."

St. Augustine

*"Love is but the discovery of ourselves in others,
and the delight in the recognition."*

Alexander Smith

"One hour of right-down love
Is worth an age of dully living on."

Aphra Behn

American Restaurant

"Sympathy constitutes friendship; but in love there is a sort of antipathy, or opposing passion. Each strives to be the other, and both together make up one whole."

Samuel Taylor Coleridge

"The richest love is that which submits to the arbitration of time."

Lawrence Durrell

"Love is, above all, the gift of oneself."

Jeane Anouilh

Café Allegro

"For where your treasure is, there your heart will be also."

Matthew 6:21

"There is only one happiness in life, to love and be loved."

George Sand, English author (1862)

"The science of love is the philosophy of the heart."

Cicero

EBT

"Love is the beauty of the soul."

St. Augustine

"I am Tarzan of the Apes. I want you. I am yours. You are mine."

Tarzan to Jane,
Wm. Rice Burroughs'
Tarzan of the Apes

"If it is your time, love will track you down like a cruise missile."

Lynda Barry,
American Humorist

Classic Cup

"The more I give to thee, the more I have, for both are infinite."

Juliet to Romeo,
Wm. Shakespeare's Romeo and Juliet

"Who travels for love finds a thousand miles not longer than one."

Japanese Proverb

Peppercorn Duck Club

Shopping, shopping, shopping!

Kansas City's *Country Club Plaza* offers a unique shopping experience. The first outdoor shopping area of its kind in the United States, the Plaza is built in the style of Seville, Spain. The Plaza's 14 blocks boast statues from around the world and some of the city's most beautiful fountains. Johnson County's answer to the Country Club Plaza, *Town Center Plaza*, is coming into its own, featuring restaurants, shops, and a movie theater. Along with the Plaza, *Crown Center* is a must see during the holiday season, with restaurants, shopping, movies, theater, and an outdoor ice skating rink. *Westport* offers specialty shops and cafes, and scattered among them are some of Kansas City's hottest nightspots. Other unique shopping locations include the *City Market, Brookside*, and a newly expanded *Oak Park Mall*.

Country Club Plaza: 47th & JC Nichols Pkwy   816-753-0100
Town Center Plaza: 119th St., between Roe & Nall   913-498-1111
Crown Center: 25th & Grand   816-274-8444
Westport: Westport Rd. & Broadway   816-756-2789

"Make me immortal with a kiss."

Dr. Faustus to Helen of Troy,
Marlowe's Dr. Faustus

FAO Schwarz

"I know one reason that kissing was created. It makes you feel warm all over, and they didn't always have electric heat or fireplaces or even stoves in their houses."

Gina, age 8

"If falling in love is anything like learning how to spell, I don't want to do it. It takes too long."

Glenn, age 7

Shopping at Crown Center

"Love is the bridge between two hearts."

Unknown

"To love another person is to see the face of God."

Les Misérables,
Andrew Lloyd Webber

SAS·CITY

Panache

Nightlife options are not in short supply in Kansas City. *The Phoenix,* downtown, offers jazz 6 nights a week. Kansas City's most popular cigar bar, *Harry's Bar and Tables*, has proven to be a worthy Westport addition. Across the street from Harry's is *Kelly's,* one of Kansas City's oldest and most popular taverns. *The Velvet Dog*, a tavern known for its martinis, has a loyal following, and offers romantic candlelight and dark corners. *The Levee*, another Kansas City landmark, offers a casual atmosphere where you can dance with your sweetheart to jazz and blues, or grab a seat outside. The *Blue Room*, located in the Kansas City Jazz Museum, also offers live jazz, and has become synonymous with the 18th and Vine district.

The Phoenix 302 W. 8th   816-472-0001
Harry's Bar and Tables: 501 Westport Rd.   816-561-3950
Kelly's: 500 Westport Rd.   816-753-9193
The Velvet Dog: 400 E. 31st   816-753-9990
The Levee: 16 W. 43rd St.   816-561-2821
The Blue Room: 1616 E. 18th   816-474-2929

"Some women blush when they are kissed, some call for the police, some swear, some bite. But the worst are those who laugh."

Unknown

Phoenix

"Love isn't like a reservoir. You'll never drain it dry. It's much more like a natural spring. The longer and the farther it flows, the stronger and the deeper and the clearer it becomes."

Eddie Cantor

"Those who love deeply never grow old; they may die of old age, but they die young."

Sir Ar

"Gravity can not be held responsible for people falling in love."

Albert Einstein

Harry's Bar and Tables

"At the touch of love everyone becomes a poet."

Plato

105

"It is impossible to love and to be wise."

Francis Bacon

The Velvet Dog

"Women are made to be loved, not understood."

Oscar Wilde

"All mankind love a lover."

Ralph Waldo Emerson

The Blue Room

Getting around Kansas City can also be romantic. Hop on one of the *Trolleys* and take a tour of some of the best Kansas City has to offer. The Trolleys cover a 16-mile loop including the Country Club Plaza, Westport, Crown Center, Downtown, and the River Market. For a more personal touch, take a ride through the Plaza in an open *horse drawn carriage*, or in one of the *"Cinderella"* carriages which surround you and your date in a pumpkin of lights. Johnson County offers 65 miles of trails that provide natural habitats for animals as well as plenty of room for jogging, biking, and fitness walking. Joggers and walkers also love *Brush Creek*, as the walkway and fountains offer a scenic and relaxing excursion from everyday worries.

The Trolley: Call for pick-up locations: 816-221-3399
Surrey's Ltd: 500 Nichols Rd   816-531-2673
Prides of Kansas City: 500 Nichols Rd.   816-531-1999
Plaza Horse and Carriage: Call for pick-up locations: 888-445-6469
Brush Creek: Wornall and Ward Parkway
Johnson County Trails: All over Shawnee Mission

"In short, my deary, kiss me, and be quiet."

Unknown

Trolley

"There is no disguise that can hide love for long where it exists, or stimulate it where it does not."

La Rochefoucauld

"Nobody has ever measured, even poets, how much the heart can hold."

Zelda Fitgerald

Horse Drawn Carriage On The Country Club Plaza

"I never knew how to worship until I knew how to love."

Henry Ward Beecher

"Love look not with the eyes, but with the mind,
and therefore is winged cupid painted blind."

$$\textit{William Shakespeare}$$

Brush Creek Walkway

"Love is composed of a single soul inhabiting two bodies."

Aristotle

"Love is the condition in which the happiness of another person is essential to your own."

Robert A. Heinlein

Cinderella Carriage

Museums and art events give Kansas City art lovers plenty to keep them satisfied. The *Nelson-Atkins Museum* of Art is renowned as Kansas City's finest art museum. One of the nation's top general art museums, the *Kemper Museum of Contemporary Art and Design*, features work by international contemporary artists in a building that itself is a piece of beautiful art. Kansas City's annual hallmark art festival, the *Plaza Art Fair*, is held at the Country Club Plaza every year over a weekend in September. The fair features artists from around the world, jazz and classical music, entertainment, and food. Other annual art festivals in Kansas City include the *Heartland National Art Festival* and *Art Westport*. For more information regarding current exhibitions and events, check the "Arts" section of the Kansas City Star.

Nelson-Atkins Museum of Art: 4525 Oak	816-751-1ART
Kemper Museum of Contemporary Art and Design:	
4420 Warwick Ave.	816-561-3737
Plaza Art Fair: Country Club Plaza	816-756-0100

"The sunlight claps the earth
And the moonbeams kiss the sea:
What are all these kissings worth
If thou kiss not me?"

Percy Bysshe Shelley

Nelson-Atkins Museum

"Love is not blind-It sees more and not less, but because it sees more it is willing to see less."

Will Moss

"Tell me whom you love and I will tell you what you are."

Arsene Houssaye

Plaza Art Fair

"Love is the triumph of imagination over intelligence."

H L Menken

"Death is a challenge. It tells us not to waste time…It tells us to tell each other right now that we love each other."

Leo F Buscaglia

Kemper Museum of Contemporary Art

Christmastime is one of the best times of year to be a Kansas Citian. The Country Club Plaza lights up every year on Thanksgiving night under hundreds of thousands of Christmas lights. In the evening, between one hundred thousand and two hundred and fifty thousand people gather to listen to a choir and sing Christmas carols. A local celebrity and a child pull the switch which turns on the *Plaza Lights*. The light display is one of the largest in the country. The following day is the mayor's *Christmas tree lighting* ceremony at Crown Center. Another way to enjoy the holiday season is to head down to the outdoor *ice skating rink,* also at Crown Center.

"A kiss on Christmas Day is the best gift a lover can give."

Unknown

Plaza Lights

"There is no remedy for love but to love more."

Thoreau

"Blushing is the color of virtue."

Diogenes

Mayor's Christmas Tree at Crown Center

"The heart is the temple wherein all truth resides."

Kahlil Gibran

"To love and win is the best thing. To love and lose, the next best."

William M. Thackery

Ice Skating at Crown Center

"That farewell kiss which resembles greeting, that last glance of love which becomes the sharpest pang of sorrow."

George Eliot

Plaza Lightpost

"...then I did the simplist thing in the world. I leaned down...and kissed him. And the world cracked open."

Agnes de Mille

Photography credits

All photography by Al Pitzner except the following:

Gary Carson: 38, 39, 44, 45, 56, 59, 104, 105

Peter Mallouk: 35, 41, 50, 91, 97

John Siebs: 94, 107, 113, 140